The Parent Challenge Workbook
By Ernesto Mejia
Assisted by Matthew Mejia
Copyright © 2019 CoolSpeak. The Youth Engagement Company.
All Rights Reserved.

Graphic and Layout Design: Iske Conradie

Book & Cover Design: Carlos Ojeda Jr.

ISBN-13: 978-0692527924

TABLE OF CONTENTS

GOAL

The goal of this workbook is providing parents with a guide to help them improve their relationships with their children by learning more about them and learning how to connect with them better.

Saving up for College – pg.14

Learn to talk – pg.5

Reconnect using letters – pg.18

1.
HOW WELL DO YOU KNOW YOUR CHILD?

To begin, take this is 10-question quiz to see how well you really know your child. Complete one for each of your children.

1. *What is your child's favorite color?*

    -

2. *Who is your child's best friend?*

    -

3. *Besides you, who has the most influence on your child's life?*

    -

4. *What does your child love most about you as a parent?*

    -

5. *What are your child's favorite subjects in school?*

    -

6. *What does you child aspire to be when he/she grows up?*

    -

7. *What is your child's username for each social media platform?*
    Facebook: -
    Twitter: -
    Instagram: -
    Snapchat: -
    WhatsApp:: -
    E-mail: -

8. *If your child could asked you for one thing, what would it be?*

    -

9. *If you told your child you had an extra $1,000.00, what would they suggest you do with it?*

    -

10. *What does your child like about school?*

    -

2.
SPENDING TIME WITH OUR CHILDREN

One of the most important things you can do as a parent is to spend time with your child. This is especially important during the most formative early years of a child's life. By giving your time to your child, you are signaling to them that they are important to you and that you recognize they deserve your love and attention.

And remember that quality is more important than quantity. Find ways to engage with your child by asking questions and sharing stories with each other.

Here are some examples of positive ways to spend time with your child:

1. *Cook/Eat together*
2. *Take family trips*
3. *Play the games they like with them*
4. *Go on one-on-one dates*
5. *Attend their games/practices/recitals/activities*
6. *Do family game nights*
7. *Do family movie nights*
8. *Organize a family picnic*
9. *Attend religious gatherings together*
10. *Go to the library/bookstore together*

General rule of thumb: **Be available when your kids need you.**

From Lifehack: Ways to Spend Time with Your Kids When You Have No Time

1. *One-on-one time:* **Alone time with your child is best when you are doing something you both enjoy. Marking your dates down on a calendar is a great idea and shows your children you make this time a priority.**
2. *Integrate together-time in your daily schedule:* **Children love to help. Invite them to assist you with daily tasks like cooking and setting the table for dinner.**
3. *Phantom time:* **Don't have a moment to spare until about 3 a.m.? You can still let your children know that you care. Write notes and drop them into your childrens' lunch boxes or tuck them under their pillows.**
4. *Break time:* **Slide in a "break time" so that you and your children can spend 15 minutes or a half hour together. Set a timer if you need to so that everyone knows when "break time" starts and finishes.**

A good way to ensure that the time you spend with your child is beneficial is to ask them what they would like to do. Your job is to interview each of your children to learn how they like to spend their time and then schedule those activities into your calendar.

Interview Questions:

1.   What is your favorite activity outside of school?

2.   What is your favorite game to play?

3.   What is your favorite book/movie/TV show?

4.   What is your favorite memory of our family spending time together?

5.   What is your favorite meal that we cook and eat at home?

6.   If we were to do a weekly family activity, what would you like to do?
     Examples: board games, movies, picnics, museums

7.   What is your favorite place you have ever traveled to?

8.   What is your favorite restaurant?

9.   What is something you have always wanted to try but never have?

3.
COMMUNICATION STYLES:
Positive vs. Degrading

Spending quality time with your child is only half of the equation. The other half is effective, positive communication. This includes daily conversations like, "How was school?". However, it also includes more difficult conversations that arise when students bring home bad grades or get suspended for fighting in school. In these moments, we must remain positive and remember never to degrade our children.

Write down some examples of your positive and negative reactions to tough parent-child scenarios:

1. Your child isn't doing his/her homework.
   Negative reaction: You yell at them and tell them they are stupid for not doing their work; hit them or ignore them.
   Positive reaction: You tell them you believe in them; ask them why they aren't doing their work so you can help remove the barriers to their success; you create a reward for completing homework and check-in regularly to make sure the work is completed.

2. *Your child is skipping school.*
   Negative reaction:
   _
   Positive reaction:
   _

3. *Your child is starting fights with kids at school and with siblings at home.*
   Negative reaction:
   _
   Positive reaction:
   _

"Be willing to forgive"

Communication Builders

1. I'd like to hear about it.
2. Tell me more about that.
3. I'm listening.
4. I understand.
5. What do you think about...?
6. Would you like to talk about it?
7. Is there anything else you'd like to talk about?
8. That's interesting.
9. I'm interested.
10. Explain that to me.

Ways To Communicate Positively With Children (from Education.com):

1. Start communicating effectively while children are young
2. Communicate at your children's level
3. *Learn to be an active listener*
   a. *Make and maintain eye contact*
   b. *Eliminate distractions*
   c. *Listen with a closed mouth and open ears*
   d. *Let your children know they have been heard by restating what they said*
4. Keep conversations brief
5. Ask the right questions
6. Express your own feelings and ideas when communicating with your children
7. Regularly schedule family meetings or times to talk
8. Admit it when you don't know something
9. Try to make explanations complete

"Admit it when you don't know something"

Communicating During Conflicts

1. Work on one problem at a time
2. Look for creative ways to solve problems
3. Be polite
4. Use "I" messages
5. Be willing to forgive

1. Nagging and lecturing
2. Interrupting
3. Criticizing
4. Dwelling on the past
5. Trying to control children through the use of guilt
6. Using sarcasm
7. Telling your children how to solve their problems
8. Putting children down
9. Using threats
10. Lying
11. Denying children's feelings

"Work on one problem at a time"

Activity Part 1

You and your child will respond to a series of questions using a talking object and the following format:

1. The person holding the talking object is the only one who may speak. The other person must listen.
2. The parent holds the talking object first to read and respond to a question.
3. The parent hands the talking object to the child.
4. The child repeats what they heard the parent say as an answer.
5. The child responds and adds to the parent's initial response.
6. Repeat for each question.

Questions:

1. What do you think it means to be a responsible person?

   -

2. Why do you think it's important to treat others with respect?

   -

3. How would you define what it means to be a successful student?

   -

4. Whose responsibility is it to maintain positive child-parent communication?

   -

5. What is one thing you will work on to improve how you communicate with your child/parent?

   -

Activity Part 2

In Part 2, both the parent and child will practice straightforward communication using honest and respectful language to give each other advice.

Child: On the lines below, write a letter to your parents explaining what they can do differently to be more helpful and supportive.

Examples:
- *It would be helpful if you did _____ more/less because...*
- *It helps me so much when you _____.*
- *I feel encouraged when you _____.*

Parent: On the lines below, write a letter to your child explaining what they can do differently to be more successful.

Examples:

- *You would benefit greatly from _____.*
- *If you did _____ more/less, your path to success would be so much easier.*
- *To be successful in your life, you should always _____.*

4.
MOTIVATING OUR CHILDREN

As a parent, you have life experience and expertise. You know what your child needs to do to succeed. You know your child needs to focus and work hard in school. Your child needs to apply to colleges and scholarships. Your child needs to have self-confidence and respect. Yet the question remains: how can we become their motivators and not their critics? A good way to begin is by assessing your relationship as a motivator as it exists right now.

Activity Part 1

Have your child circle one of the numbers 1–5 to rate you on a scale from Critic to Motivator. Then, have them answer the questions below.

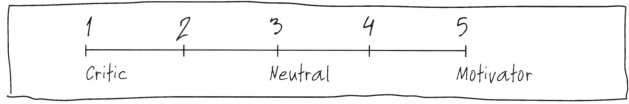

1. *Why did you rate your parent the way you did?*

   -
   -
   -

2. *Describe a specific time when your parent criticized you, but did not motivate you.*

   -
   -
   -

3. *Given who you are and your personality, how can your parents better motivate you?*

   -
   -
   -

Activity Part 2

Read each of the questions to your child one at a time. Allow them to read and explain their responses after you read each question. After listening to each of their responses, discuss and respond from your point of view in a patient and respectful manner.

5.
RAISING INDEPENDENT THINKERS

In today's workplace, independent thinkers are the most valued employees and leaders. An important sign of an independent thinker is the ability to solve one's problems. In a 2013 article, Forbes listed "Ability to make decisions and solve problems" as the second most important skill employers seek ("ability to work in a team" is first). The reason is simple: independent thinkers don't need someone there to hold their hand and make every little decision for them.

If you want to make sure you are raising an independent thinker, follow the four areas Education.com lists as vital to their growth. Work on these areas with your child:

1. *Talk:* *Encourage your child to talk in descriptive terms.*
2. *Listen:* *Engage your child's listening skills, and teach him/her how to pay attention to what others are saying before sharing his/her own thoughts on the matter.*
3. *Think:* *Encourage your child to try and solve their own problems instead of solving it for them.*
4. *Write:* *You can start with your child practicing how to tell stories verbally, but it's important that it progresses into written form thereafter.*

Activity

Here you will find a classic and simple game that will help you practice creative problem solving and promote independent thinking in your child.

The problem:

Draw four straight lines through the nine dots without retracing a line and without lifting your pen from the paper. Try a few different methods on the three blocks below. Turn the page for possible solutions.

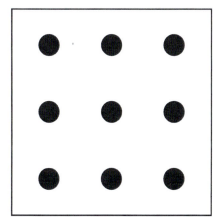
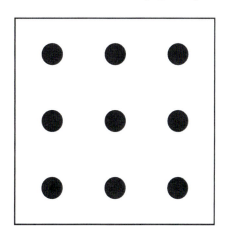
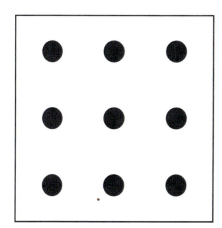

The key to the solution is, of course, that the imaginary boundaries formed by the dots need not be observed. Once freed from this restriction, you will find the solution easy, as shown here.

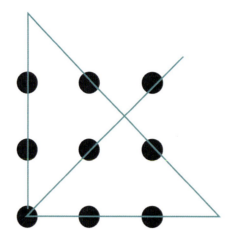

Researchers at Stanford University have come up with an even more interesting solution to this puzzle. One subject realized that it wasn't necessary to draw four lines through the centers of the dots; the problem can be solved with only three lines.

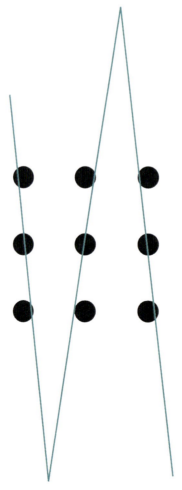

6.
COMMUNICATING WITH SCHOOL OFFICIALS

As a parent, you are the most important advocate in your child's life. This is especially true when it comes to their schooling. In order to empower yourself as your child's advocate, you need to know how to effectively communicate with various school officials. While all school officials should always be ready to speak and work with you to address your concerns, you should reach out to different people for different reasons. Some examples are listed below:

- *Teachers:* **Contact them for any issues occurring within their classroom, whether unsatisfactory grades, bullying, or anything in-between;**
- *Guidance Counselors:* **Contact them in the case of social/emotional concerns, as well as anything related to class scheduling and college applications;**
- *Dean of Students:* **Contact the Dean for any issues requiring disciplinary action;**
- *Principal:* **Contact your principal when other school leaders can't meet your needs to a satisfactory degree.**

Ways to get involved

There are a few good ways to get involved in your child's education. A good start is joining your school's Parent-Teacher Association (PTA). This is an effective way for parents to organize and communicate with teachers and school leaders. Additionally, you can...

- *Volunteer in the classroom;*
- *Chaperon a class field trip;*
- *Help construct the set and costumes for a school play;*
- *Be the advisor for a school club;*
- *Coach or assist a school sports team;*
- *Help create decorations for school dances/events.*

All of these are ways not only to play an active role in your student's educational experience, but they also serve as a way to build relationships with other parents and leaders in your child's school. When other parent and school leaders see you around, they will know who your child is, and they will be more likely to invest their time in him/her. Additionally, these types of relationships will serve you and your child well when it comes time to ask for something like a recommendation letter or a summer job/internship.

Activity

Ask your child what school activities they plan to participate in this year, and then come up with at least three ways you will actively engage in your child's academic experience in the coming school year.

1. _____

2. _____

3. _____

7.
SAVING/PAYING FOR COLLEGE

For most parents, this is the most daunting aspect of sending a child to college. It's not uncommon for you to think, "Yes, college sounds nice, but how in the world am I going to pay for that?" Hopefully after this session, you will feel equipped and empowered to send your child to any school of their choosing.

The key is to start planning and saving early. You need to know your options and plan accordingly. Also know that college is a realistic option, and that while it is typically worth the debt of student loans, they may not be necessary if you put in the work ahead of time.

Below, the following items are addressed:

A.   *529 College Savings Plan*
B.   *Applying for FAFSA*
C.   *Types of Student Loans*
D.   *HACER Scholarship*

A.   529 College Savings Plan

What is a 529 plan?

Whether you're a new parent, grandparent or a prospective student, a 529 plan can help you effectively save for college. Just like a retirement account, these investment vehicles combine the power of compound interest with federal tax benefits, creating the potential for substantial growth over time. And since they are administered by the states, you may also be eligible for additional state tax benefits. Families of all income levels can enjoy the benefits of 529 plans, with no annual contribution limits and monthly contribution minimums as low as $25.

For a video introduction to 529 plans, visit ***www.coolspeak.net/resources/parent-resources.***
For detailed information on 529 plans, including state-by-state benefit comparisons, what can be considered a "qualified expense," and enrollment instructions, visit ***www.coolspeak.net/resources/parent-resources.***

B.   Applying for FAFSA

What is Federal Student Aid?

From the FAFSA "about" page:
Federal Student Aid, a part of the US Department of Education, is the largest provider of student financial aid in the nation. The office of Federal Student Aid provides grants, loans, and work-study funds for college or career school. They offer more than $150 billion each year to help millions of students pay for higher education.

Where do I complete the FAFSA?

You can complete the FAFSA form online at ***fafsa.ed.gov.*** It is available in English and Spanish.
Visit ***www.coolspeak.net/resources/parent-resources*** for details on the deadlines.

What do I need to complete my Free Application for Federal Student Aid?

1.   *Social Security Number (if applicable)*

2.   *Permanent Resident Card (if applicable)*
3.   *W-2 forms or other records of money earned for the previous year*
4.   *Tax records*

What resources can help me with the FAFSA process and finding the right loans for me?

At any point during the application process, you can click on a "Help" button for assistance and to request a live online chat with a Federal Student Aid agent. In addition, the "FederalStudentAid" channel on YouTube has very helpful video tutorials for the application and repayment processes. On ***www.youtube.com*** search "***FederalStudentAid***" to find this channel with playlists including:

- *Prepare for College*
- *FAFSA: Apply for Aid*
- *Who Gets Aid*
- *Types of Aid*
- *Repay Your Loans*

For detailed information on the various types of federal loans available, visit ***www.coolspeak.net/resources/parent-resources.***

C.   Types of Student Loans

What is the difference between federal and private student loans?

There are two main differences between federal and private student loans:

- *Interest Rates: Federal student loans tend to have significantly lower and more stable interest rates than student loans from private lenders.*
- *Repayment Options: Federal student loans tend to have much more flexible repayment options than student loans from private lenders.*

Which type of loan is better?

The lower interest rates and more flexible repayment options make federal student loans more desirable than private student loans. However, not everyone is eligible for federal student loans, and federal student loans do not always cover a student's full cost of tuition, room and board, etc. Because of this, families will often combine federal and private student loans. When doing this, be mindful of these differences when interacting with your lenders.

Help your child complete the guide below to begin creating a game plan for getting into college.

1. In what areas of study are you most interested?

2. What colleges (or types of colleges) best fit your areas of interest?

3. How do you plan to save and/or pay for college?

4. List your favorite extracurricular activities you could do with your parents.

5. List some colleges you would like to visit on family trips.

6. What are some of your fears about going to college?

- -
- -
- -
- -

7. How will you, as a college graduate, help your parents when you're making some money?

- -
- -
- -
- -

8.
OUR JOURNAL

A very powerful way for parents and children to communicate with one another is to write to each other. And we're not talking about text messages and e-mails here. We're talking good old-fashioned handwritten notes and letters. A parent's words of encouragement are always welcomed and appreciated by their children.

But a handwritten note brings those words into the physical world and gives them a life beyond the moment they are uttered. A letter from mom can be read time and again to give strength and courage during a difficult time. Likewise, a handwritten note can warm the heart of a father that aches to see his daughter who is away at college.

Activity

To practice writing to one another, use the lines below to respond to the prompt provided. Then read and compare your responses together.

Our Vision of the Future: Write a letter to your parent describing what life will be like after you graduate from college and find a good career.

Our Vision of the Future: Write a letter to your child describing what life will be like after he/she graduates from college and finds a good career.

9.
THE IMPORTANCE OF STRUCTURE
– *We are their first teachers.*

As parents, you are the first and most important example for your children. They will learn their earliest and longest lasting habits from you, so you need to set a good example for them. All parents want their children to have a bright future, but to make that happen, you must teach them how to behave, react, and communicate. You must teach them these habits for success.

Activity Part 1

List the 5 most important habits you think your child needs to succeed in school and in life.

1. _____
2. _____
3. _____
4. _____
5. _____

Activity Part 2

For each of the habits you listed above, describe one way you set a good example for your child and one way you could improve the example you set. Examples could be seeing parents read, exercise, eat at the table, NOT watch TV, NOT be on their cell phones.

1. *Good example:* _____
   Focus for improvement: _____
2. *Good example:* _____
   Focus for improvement: _____
3. *Good example:* _____
   Focus for improvement: _____
4. *Good example:* _____
   Focus for improvement: _____
5. *Good example:* _____
   Focus for improvement: _____

Another way to build good habits is to create structure through rules and schedules. Below are some tips and links to resources for creating rules and building structure around a daily schedule, family rules, and household chores.

Creating Structure and Rules

Keys to Creating Structure

1. *Consistency, predictability, and follow-through are important for creating structure in the home.*
2. *Respond to your child's behavior the same way every time. When you are consistent, the behaviors you like will happen more often and problem behaviors are less likely to happen.*
3. *Routines and daily schedules help you and your child. You both know what to expect each day. Routines can also improve your child's behavior and your relationship with your child.*
4. *A family rule is a clear statement about behaviors that are never okay, such as hitting and running in the house. You can change your child's behavior when there are clear consequences for breaking the rule.*
5. *Keep things positive! Reward and praise your child for following routines and rules. This makes it more likely that your child will follow the routines and rules in the future.*

Daily Schedule

Create a daily schedule that fits the needs of your family. Think about the activities you want your children to participate in. Put the activities in the order they will happen. Try to keep the schedule similar from day to day.

Download a PDF daily schedule template right here: **www.coolspeak.net/resources/parent-resources.**

Family Rules

A family rule is a specific, clear statement of what you expect. Create a list of your family's core rules so your family has a clear understanding of what is okay and what is not okay.

Download a PDF template for your family rule right here: **www.coolspeak.net/resources/parent-resources.**

My Chore Chart

Letting your child know what you expect is important for a positive parent-child relationship. On this core chart, list the daily expectations for how your child will contribute to your household. Remember to keep your expectations appropriate for your child's age.

Download a PDF chore chart template right here: **www.coolspeak.net/resources/parent-resources.**

10.
THE PARENT HABIT CHALLENGE

As you conclude this workbook, you are faced with a challenge. Based on what you have learned today, what will you change in your life to become a better parent and to set your child up for success?

In the following pages, you will find copies of a 28-day Parent Habit Challenge calendar. Each of them has space for you to identify up to three habits you wish to change over the next four weeks. On the lines in the boxes, you can write daily notes about whether it was a successful day or whether you had some trouble sticking to your pledge to improve. We included multiple copies in case you have multiple children. We encourage you to use one calendar per child.

If you need help thinking of which habits you would like to focus on, refer back to what you wrote in Part 2 of the activity in the previous section. That will help to guide you in determining where you should focus your efforts for self-improvement as a parent.

THE PARENT
HABIT CHALLENGE

Start date: _ _ _ _ _ _ _ Finish date: _ _ _ _ _ _ Goal 1: _ _ _ _ _ _ Goal 2: _ _ _ _ _ _ Goal 3: _ _ _ _ _

☐☐☐ Day 1
Note: _ _ _ _ _ _ _ _
_ _ _ _ _ _ _ _
_ _ _ _ _ _ _ _
_ _ _ _ _ _ _ _
_ _ _ _ _ _ _ _
_ _ _ _ _ _ _ _

☐☐☐ Day 2
Note: _ _ _ _ _ _ _ _
_ _ _ _ _ _ _ _
_ _ _ _ _ _ _ _
_ _ _ _ _ _ _ _
_ _ _ _ _ _ _ _
_ _ _ _ _ _ _ _

☐☐☐ Day 3
Note: _ _ _ _ _ _ _ _
_ _ _ _ _ _ _ _
_ _ _ _ _ _ _ _
_ _ _ _ _ _ _ _
_ _ _ _ _ _ _ _
_ _ _ _ _ _ _ _

☐☐☐ Day 4
Note: _ _ _ _ _ _ _ _

☐☐☐ Day 5
Note: _ _ _ _ _ _ _ _

☐☐☐ Day 6
Note: _ _ _ _ _ _ _ _

☐☐☐ Day 7
Note: _ _ _ _ _ _ _ _

☐☐☐ Day 8
Note: _ _ _ _ _ _ _ _

☐☐☐ Day 9
Note: _ _ _ _ _ _ _ _

☐☐☐ Day 10
Note: _ _ _ _ _ _ _ _

☐☐☐ Day 11
Note: _ _ _ _ _ _ _ _

☐☐☐ Day 12
Note: _ _ _ _ _ _ _ _

☐☐☐ Day 13
Note: _ _ _ _ _ _ _ _

☐☐☐ Day 14
Note: _ _ _ _ _ _ _ _

☐☐☐ Day 15
Note: _ _ _ _ _ _ _ _

☐☐☐ Day 16
Note: _ _ _ _ _ _ _ _

☐☐☐ Day 17
Note: _ _ _ _ _ _ _ _

☐☐☐ Day 18
Note: _ _ _ _ _ _ _ _

☐☐☐ Day 19
Note: _ _ _ _ _ _ _ _

☐☐☐ Day 20
Note: _ _ _ _ _ _ _ _

☐☐☐ Day 21
Note: _ _ _ _ _ _ _ _

☐☐☐ Day 22
Note: _ _ _ _ _ _ _ _

☐☐☐ Day 23
Note: _ _ _ _ _ _ _ _

☐☐☐ Day 24
Note: _ _ _ _ _ _ _ _

☐☐☐ Day 25
Note: _ _ _ _ _ _ _ _

☐☐☐ Day 26
Note: _ _ _ _ _ _ _ _

☐☐☐ Day 27
Note: _ _ _ _ _ _ _ _

☐☐☐ Day 28
Note: _ _ _ _ _ _ _ _

THE PARENT HABIT CHALLENGE

Start date: _____ Finish date: _____ Goal 1: _____ Goal 2: _____ Goal 3: _____

☐☐☐ Day 1
Note: _____

☐☐☐ Day 2
Note: _____

☐☐☐ Day 3
Note: _____

☐☐☐ Day 4
Note: _____

☐☐☐ Day 5
Note: _____

☐☐☐ Day 6
Note: _____

☐☐☐ Day 7
Note: _____

☐☐☐ Day 8
Note: _____

☐☐☐ Day 9
Note: _____

☐☐☐ Day 10
Note: _____

☐☐☐ Day 11
Note: _____

☐☐☐ Day 12
Note: _____

☐☐☐ Day 13
Note: _____

☐☐☐ Day 14
Note: _____

☐☐☐ Day 15
Note: _____

☐☐☐ Day 16
Note: _____

☐☐☐ Day 17
Note: _____

☐☐☐ Day 18
Note: _____

☐☐☐ Day 19
Note: _____

☐☐☐ Day 20
Note: _____

☐☐☐ Day 21
Note: _____

☐☐☐ Day 22
Note: _____

☐☐☐ Day 23
Note: _____

☐☐☐ Day 24
Note: _____

☐☐☐ Day 25
Note: _____

☐☐☐ Day 26
Note: _____

☐☐☐ Day 27
Note: _____

☐☐☐ Day 28
Note: _____

coolspeak.
The Youth Engagement Company

WWW.COOLSPEAK.NET

THE PARENT
HABIT CHALLENGE

Start date: _____   Finish date: _____   Goal 1: _____   Goal 2: _____   Goal 3: _____

☐☐☐ Day 1	☐☐☐ Day 2	☐☐☐ Day 3	☐☐☐ Day 4	☐☐☐ Day 5	☐☐☐ Day 6	☐☐☐ Day 7
Note:	Note:	Note:	Note:	Note:	Note:	Note:

☐☐☐ Day 8	☐☐☐ Day 9	☐☐☐ Day 10	☐☐☐ Day 11	☐☐☐ Day 12	☐☐☐ Day 13	☐☐☐ Day 14
Note:	Note:	Note:	Note:	Note:	Note:	Note:

☐☐☐ Day 15	☐☐☐ Day 16	☐☐☐ Day 17	☐☐☐ Day 18	☐☐☐ Day 19	☐☐☐ Day 20	☐☐☐ Day 21
Note:	Note:	Note:	Note:	Note:	Note:	Note:

☐☐☐ Day 22	☐☐☐ Day 23	☐☐☐ Day 24	☐☐☐ Day 25	☐☐☐ Day 26	☐☐☐ Day 27	☐☐☐ Day 28
Note:	Note:	Note:	Note:	Note:	Note:	Note:

THE PARENT
HABIT CHALLENGE

Start date: _ _ _ _ _ _ _ Finish date: _ _ _ _ _ _ _ Goal 1: _ _ _ _ _ _ _ Goal 2: _ _ _ _ _ _ _ Goal 3: _ _ _ _ _ _ _

☐☐☐ Day 1
Note: _ _ _ _ _ _ _ _ _ _ _ _ _ _ _ _ _

☐☐☐ Day 2
Note: _ _ _ _ _ _ _ _ _ _ _ _ _ _ _ _ _

☐☐☐ Day 3
Note: _ _ _ _ _ _ _ _ _ _ _ _ _ _ _ _ _

☐☐☐ Day 4
Note: _ _ _ _ _ _ _ _ _ _ _ _ _ _ _ _ _

☐☐☐ Day 5
Note: _ _ _ _ _ _ _ _ _ _ _ _ _ _ _ _ _

☐☐☐ Day 6
Note: _ _ _ _ _ _ _ _ _ _ _ _ _ _ _ _ _

☐☐☐ Day 7
Note: _ _ _ _ _ _ _ _ _ _ _ _ _ _ _ _ _

☐☐☐ Day 8
Note: _ _ _ _ _ _ _ _ _ _ _ _ _ _ _ _ _

☐☐☐ Day 9
Note: _ _ _ _ _ _ _ _ _ _ _ _ _ _ _ _ _

☐☐☐ Day 10
Note: _ _ _ _ _ _ _ _ _ _ _ _ _ _ _ _ _

☐☐☐ Day 11
Note: _ _ _ _ _ _ _ _ _ _ _ _ _ _ _ _ _

☐☐☐ Day 12
Note: _ _ _ _ _ _ _ _ _ _ _ _ _ _ _ _ _

☐☐☐ Day 13
Note: _ _ _ _ _ _ _ _ _ _ _ _ _ _ _ _ _

☐☐☐ Day 14
Note: _ _ _ _ _ _ _ _ _ _ _ _ _ _ _ _ _

☐☐☐ Day 15
Note: _ _ _ _ _ _ _ _ _ _ _ _ _ _ _ _ _

☐☐☐ Day 16
Note: _ _ _ _ _ _ _ _ _ _ _ _ _ _ _ _ _

☐☐☐ Day 17
Note: _ _ _ _ _ _ _ _ _ _ _ _ _ _ _ _ _

☐☐☐ Day 18
Note: _ _ _ _ _ _ _ _ _ _ _ _ _ _ _ _ _

☐☐☐ Day 19
Note: _ _ _ _ _ _ _ _ _ _ _ _ _ _ _ _ _

☐☐☐ Day 20
Note: _ _ _ _ _ _ _ _ _ _ _ _ _ _ _ _ _

☐☐☐ Day 21
Note: _ _ _ _ _ _ _ _ _ _ _ _ _ _ _ _ _

☐☐☐ Day 22
Note: _ _ _ _ _ _ _ _ _ _ _ _ _ _ _ _ _

☐☐☐ Day 23
Note: _ _ _ _ _ _ _ _ _ _ _ _ _ _ _ _ _

☐☐☐ Day 24
Note: _ _ _ _ _ _ _ _ _ _ _ _ _ _ _ _ _

☐☐☐ Day 25
Note: _ _ _ _ _ _ _ _ _ _ _ _ _ _ _ _ _

☐☐☐ Day 26
Note: _ _ _ _ _ _ _ _ _ _ _ _ _ _ _ _ _

☐☐☐ Day 27
Note: _ _ _ _ _ _ _ _ _ _ _ _ _ _ _ _ _

☐☐☐ Day 28
Note: _ _ _ _ _ _ _ _ _ _ _ _ _ _ _ _ _

THE PARENT
HABIT CHALLENGE

Start date: _ _ _ _ _   Finish date: _ _ _ _ _   Goal 1: _ _ _ _ _   Goal 2: _ _ _ _ _   Goal 3: _ _ _ _ _

☐☐☐ Day 1 Note:	☐☐☐ Day 2 Note:	☐☐☐ Day 3 Note:	☐☐☐ Day 4 Note:	☐☐☐ Day 5 Note:	☐☐☐ Day 6 Note:	☐☐☐ Day 7 Note:
☐☐ Day 8 Note:	☐☐☐ Day 9 Note:	☐☐☐ Day 10 Note:	☐☐☐ Day 11 Note:	☐☐☐ Day 12 Note:	☐☐☐ Day 13 Note:	☐☐☐ Day 14 Note:
☐☐ Day 15 Note:	☐☐☐ Day 16 Note:	☐☐☐ Day 17 Note:	☐☐☐ Day 18 Note:	☐☐☐ Day 19 Note:	☐☐☐ Day 20 Note:	☐☐☐ Day 21 Note:
☐☐ Day 22 Note:	☐☐☐ Day 23 Note:	☐☐☐ Day 24 Note:	☐☐☐ Day 25 Note:	☐☐☐ Day 26 Note:	☐☐☐ Day 27 Note:	☐☐☐ Day 28 Note:

11.
FAMILY HISTORY QUIZ

Directions: Ask your children to take this quiz.

Review their answers, for the ones they knew, revisit those stories. For the ones they didn't, take the opportunity to share stories that will strengthen their sense of family and identity, all while helping make deeper connections with them.

1. Where did your parents meet?
2. Why do your parents live where they do?
3. What was it like for your parents growing up?
4. What were your grandparents like with your parents?
5. What was the day like when you were born? What was the day after your birth like?
6. What were your parents' likes, interest, and hobbies when they were in high school?
7. What is your parents' favorite memory of you?
8. Where are our ancestors from?
9. What did your parents wish for you when you were a kid?
10. What kind of music did your parents listen to in high school?

Directions: Now you and your kids can come up with some of your own questions.

- -
- -
- -
- -
- -
- -
- -
- -
- -
- -

12.
THE PARENT CHALLENGE
COLLEGE PREP CHECKLIST

Freshman:

☐ 1. Help your child start good school habits like having a study schedule, being involved in school and talking to their teachers on a regular basis.

☐ 2. Encourage your child to sign up for advanced and honors courses.

☐ 3. Create a folder to keep a record of all accomplishments and recognitions your child receives over their entire high school career.

☐ 4. Start researching with your child what career paths may be in high demand 8 years from now.

☐ 5. Ensure your child gets involved in a club or organization at school.

☐ 6. Encourage your child to try different things such as clubs, classes, or after school programs.

☐ 7. Have your child talk to a Senior about what they did well and would have done better.

☐ 8. Encourage your child to seek out volunteer opportunities so they can get their hours done early.

☐ 9. Encourage your child to work with their counselor to plan out all 4 years of high school coursework.

☐ 10. Have your child write themselves a graduation letter with a list of goals they hope to accomplish in the next 4 years. Extra Credit: Write a graduation letter for your child focusing on how proud of them you are on that special day. Keep it and share on that special day.

For sophomores:

☐ 1. Ask your child what they want to do after high school?

☐ 2. Have your child practice standardized testing early on. (https://collegereadiness.collegeboard.org/sat/practice) (https://www.number2.com/)

☐ 3. Get your child to start with volunteer work, job shadowing and/or interning.

☐ 4. Have your child take a personality or career assessment. (https://www.careeronestop.org/)

☐ 5. Start a list of colleges/universities your child is interested in attending and research them.

☐ 6. Continue ensuring your child's involved at school i.e. clubs, organizations, with volunteer work and with after-school programs etc.

☐ 7. Start creating a scholarship hit-list.

☐ 8. Create a vision board with your child about their passions, who they want to be and what they want to do. Put it up in the house where you can all see his or her dreams.

☐ 9. Take your child on a college visit to get accustomed to how they look and work.

☐ 10. Search for a summer enrichment/camp opportunities for your child.

For Juniors:

- [ ] 1. Begin preparing for a successful Junior and Senior year.
- [ ] 2. Schedule your child's standardized tests in advance (SAT & ACT)
- [ ] 3. Have your child continue with volunteering, job shadowing or interning.
- [ ] 4. Have your child talk with their teachers about their academic goals and request their support.
- [ ] 5. Start narrowing down your child's top 10 colleges/universities.
- [ ] 6. Encourage your child to begin taking college courses whenever possible.
- [ ] 7. Schedule multiple campus tours.
- [ ] 8. Ensure your child stays involved in school i.e. clubs, organizations, volunteering, after-school programs, etc.
- [ ] 9. Update your student file of achievements i.e. awards, recognition, newspaper articles, thank you letters etc.
- [ ] 10. Search for a summer enrichment/camp opportunity and/or summer job for your child.

For Seniors:

- [ ] 1. Have your child take, or retake, all standardized tests as it could help you obtain a scholarship!
- [ ] 2. Make sure your child meets with their high school counselor to ensure they are on track to graduate.
- [ ] 3. Have you child ask teachers, counselors, coaches, or employers for reference letters for admissions and scholarships.
- [ ] 4. Have your child fill out the common college application.
- [ ] 5. Help your child narrow their school choices to their top 5 and one emergency backup option and apply to all the schools. Allow them to select their school of choice, not yours, but theirs.
- [ ] 6. Complete the FAFSA application by October 1. Then review the FAFSA Student Aid Report once it arrives.
- [ ] 7. When possible schedule an unofficial visit to your child's college/university of choice to ensure you feel comfortable on that campus.
- [ ] 8. Help your child to apply for a minimum of 75 different scholarships.
- [ ] 9. Help your child to avoid senioritis and finish strong so their school doesn't rescind their offer. You can do this by encouraging them and revisiting the vision board you made together during their sophomore year.
- [ ] 10. Have your child thank his / her teachers, counselors, and everyone necessary for their support in making their educational goals a reality!
- [ ] 11. BONUS: have your child read the letter they wrote to themselves as a freshman. This will help them see whether they accomplished all of their goals. Then give them the letter you wrote them in their freshman year.

Made in the USA
Middletown, DE
09 November 2024

64056273R00020